A Thankful Book for Kids

A Thankful Book for Kids

Giving Thanks, Helping Others, and Feeling Grateful

By Stacey Freeman, PhD

Illustrations by Letícia Moreno

ROCKRIDGE
PRESS

For general information on our other products and services, please contact our Customer Care Department within the United States at (866) 744-2665, or outside the United States at (510) 253-0500.

Paperback ISBN: 978-1-68539-098-3
eBook ISBN: 978-1-68539-482-0

Manufactured in the United States of America

Interior and Cover Designer: Gabe Nansen
Art Producer: Melissa Malinowksy
Editor: Laura Bryn Sisson
Production Editor: Nora Milman
Production Manager: Lanore Coloprisco

Illustration © 2022 Letícia Moreno
Author photo courtesy of Jade Freeman, Posh in Progress

10 9 8 7 6 5 4 3 2 1

For Rocco and Gigi:
I am so thankful I am your mommy.

You are getting so big!
You can do so many new things.

But sometimes
you still need help from
other people.

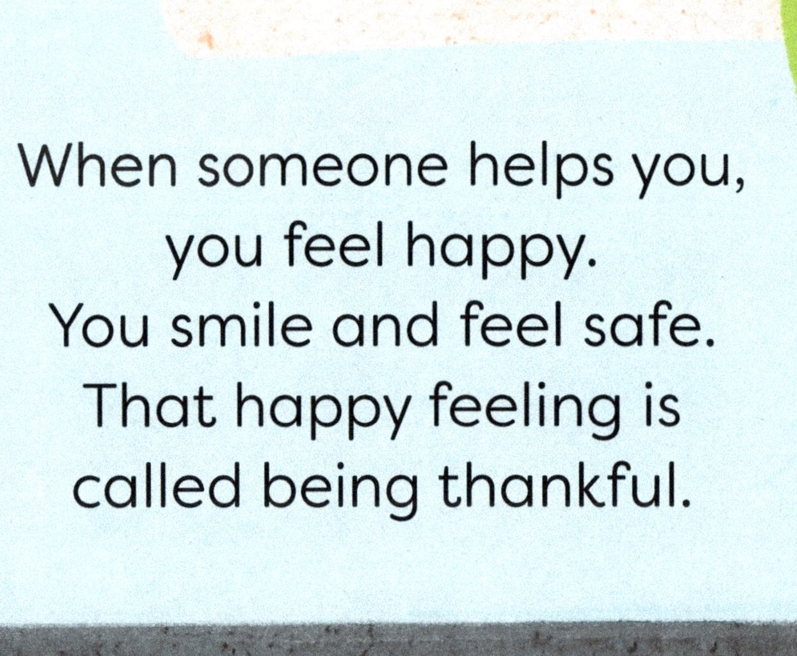

When someone helps you,
you feel happy.
You smile and feel safe.
That happy feeling is
called being thankful.

BANK

When you are thankful,
you feel warm and fuzzy.
Thankfulness feels good in your body,
just like getting a big hug.

If you need help, you can ask
nicely and say "please."
When someone helps you,
it is kind to say "thank you."

There are many ways
to show you are thankful
without using words.
You can show you are thankful
through your actions.

When someone helps you,
you can give them your
biggest smile.
They will *see* you are thankful.

Puzzle

You can give the person
who helped you a giant bear hug
(as long as they say it's okay).
They will *feel* you are thankful.

After someone helps you,
you can give them a gift,
like flowers you picked yourself.
They will *smell* you are thankful!

Sometimes you might have things
other people don't.
It feels good to be thankful
for what you have.

Sharing is a way to show your thankfulness. It is kind to share with your friends.

You are coloring in your favorite
coloring book. Your friend doesn't
have one, so you share one of the
pictures and crayons with
your friend.

You love to swing, but your friend
hasn't gotten a turn.
You ask your friend if they
want a turn.

When someone shares with you,
it is nice to say "thank you"!
It feels good to tell people you are
thankful for their friendship.

Being thankful is a feeling,
but it's also something
you can choose to do.
You can be thankful every day.
Being thankful for your life
makes you feel happy.

You can be thankful
for feeling the soft grass
between your toes
as you run barefoot.

You can be thankful
for spending time with
your grandma.

You can be thankful for all the people in your life who take care of you and show you kindness and love.

You're growing up, and
you're learning about yourself
and your feelings.
Being thankful is one of
those feelings.

HOW I FEEL TODAY
happy
sad
scared
tired
angry
thankful
nervous
confused

Remember, when you are thankful, you can show people through your actions and tell them with your words. You are thankful!

A Note to Grown-ups

Toddler Development and Thankfulness

As your toddler grows, they will experience more emotions. If your toddler feels comfortable talking about their emotions, they will feel more emotionally secure and develop empathy, kindness, and compassion. Toddlers learn behavior by watching the people around them. They also behave based on the cues and rules they've been taught and will behave differently depending on what motivates them. If your child understands why it is good to be thankful, they will be more motivated to feel and express thankfulness. Toddlers learn by watching you, so they can learn thankfulness by watching you model the behavior for them.

How to Model Thankfulness for Children

Here are more tips for how to teach toddlers thankfulness.

Model thankfulness every day. If your toddler helps pick up their toys, you can say "thank you" and explain why you appreciate what they did.

When your toddler shows thankfulness, you can *praise* them. If they say "thank you" when you serve them breakfast, say "you're welcome" and tell them you appreciate their thanks.

Help your toddler *practice* saying "please" and "thank you." If they don't remember to say one of these phrases, remind them that it is kind to say "please" and "thank you" when someone helps them.

Talk about the things for which you are thankful. If it's a lovely day, talk about how thankful you are for the sunshine. If you get a promotion at work, talk about how thankful you are for the new opportunity. Expressing gratitude every day is a wonderful way to model thankfulness.

ABOUT THE AUTHOR

Stacey Freeman holds a PhD in educational policy and evaluation. She is the executive director of a research institute focused on kindness. For the past seventeen years, she has directed university education and outreach programs, working with schools and after-school programs in the United States, and children's and science museums around the world. She is the editor in chief of PoshInProgress.com, a lifestyle blog focused on parenting, fashion, travel, and recipes. Stacey lives in Los Angeles with her children, Rocco and Gigi.

ABOUT THE ILLUSTRATOR

Letícia Moreno is an Afro-Brazilian illustrator from Rio de Janeiro, Brazil. She graduated in Art History at the School of Fine Arts of the Federal University of Rio de Janeiro (EBA/UFRJ). Her work focuses on using bold colors and textures to create fun pieces through illustration. When not drawing you will surely find Letícia either playing Animal Crossing, making some vegan recipes, or playing with her dogs, Soshi and Pimenta.